Railroads of The Hudson River Valley
1979-2008

By Bill Mc Bride

First Printing • December 2008

ISBN 978-0-615-26470-7

Softbound $45.00 U.S.

Individual copies postpaid by mail from the author
19 Amalfi Drive,
Cortlandt Manor, NY 10567

Also available at selected book retailers.

Design and Layout: Tom Nemeth

Printed by GRIT Commercial Printing, Montoursville, PA USA

Printed and Bound in The United States of America

ABOVE: Canadian Pacific (D&H) has overhead rights on the Hudson Line between Albany and Fresh Pond Jct. In Queens. They exercise these rights on an as-needed basis, usually about three times a week. Only during the longest days of the year does one have the opportunity to photograph this otherwise nocturnal train. On May 23, 2007, about a dozen railfan photographers gathered at Dobbs Ferry, NY, to photograph this pair of SD40-2's on the evening northbound when rumors circulated that CP was abdicating their agreement and this would be their last run on the Hudson Line. Like Mark Twain, the reports of their death was premature.   Dobbs Ferry, NY, May 2007

Dedication

To Suzanne, my wife of 43 years,
whose encouragement and enthusiasm is infectious.

Hers is not a tacit acceptance of my love of railroads;
she has made it a family celebration.

Railroads of The Hudson River Valley
1979 — 2008

This book is a celebration of the countless hours I have spent trackside on both banks of the Hudson River between Albany, New York, and New York City. The frequency and diversity of trains, set against the backdrop of sheer beauty known as the Hudson River Valley, was my impetus to return day after day, location after location, to record it all in photographs. I still do. The valley and its railroads have not lost their appeal. In this publication, I strive not only to share my photographs with the reader, but my endeavors and adventures to get those photographs.

The Hudson River Valley is still a magnet that attracts railfan photographers from all over our country. There is still excitement and beauty on both banks of the Mighty Hudson, as CSX, Metro North and Amtrak polish the rails daily. What has been written off as gone, is not truly gone, because it lives on within the covers of this book. Enjoy!

Bill Mc Bride
Cortlandt Manor, NY

December 2008

OPPOSITE: CSX SD40-2 8095 leads a stack train south through Iona Island. It is seen at MP 40, at the far southern end of the Island.
Iona Island, NY, June 2006

The West Shore — Colonie to Selkirk

Although the Hudson River has its origin in the middle of the Adirondack Park Forest Preserve, near the town of Tahawus in Essex County, big time railroading in the Hudson River Valley actually starts near the cities of Albany, Rensselaer and Colonie, about 110 miles to the south. The Delaware & Hudson Railway's shop in Colonie, N.Y. suffered a major fire in 2004 and was demolished. The D&H Railway ceased to be when it was purchased by Guilford Transportation in 1984, and declared bankruptcy a short time later. In 1991 it was absorbed into Canadian Pacific. CP maintains a yard in the Port of Albany, but the Delaware & Hudson Railway in now just a fond memory.

Today, Amtrak's Rensselaer Shops, the Port of Albany, and CSX's Selkirk Yard anchor the railroad scene in the Upper Hudson River Valley area.

ABOVE: Alco RS-3 4075 sits outside of the shop building on a mild Ides of March. I gave myself a birthday treat that day, by making a pleasant spring drive up to the D&H from Ossining, NY. Colonie, NY, March 1979

OPPOSITE TOP: A D&H train is seen crossing the Hudson River just north of Mechanicville, NY, without so much as a glance from the two boaters. The power lash up is U23-B 2316, GP39-2 7401, GP38-2 7324 and GP39-2 7404. Riverside, NY, September 1983

OPPOSITE BOTTOM: On a very cold day in January 1982, I showed up at the main gate of the D&H Colonie shops and, uncharacteristically, had a difficult time gaining admittance. I was beginning to think that the trip had been a mistake, when someone who recognized me from prior visits ushered me in. Idling in front of the shop was RS-11 5005 and RS-36 5021. Amazing how a couple of Alcos can change your disposition! Colonie, NY, January 1982

OPPOSITE TOP: Inside the hallowed halls of the D&H Colonie shops. Opened in 1912, the shops were abandoned in the mid-1990's. In 2004, vandals set fire to the structure, which resulted in its demolition. Here, in better days, GE U33-C 661 is among the units being serviced.
Colonie, NY, April 1986

OPPOSITE BOTTOM: The dedicated and exceptionally talented workforce at Colonie could accomplish any kind of repair. The diesel smoke was thick the day I had the opportunity to take these photos. Most of the photography was taken from the loft, high above the work floor, where the smoke was concentrated. I don't think I have ever suffered a worse headache, but I am quite sure you will agree; it was worth it!
Colonie, NY, April 1986

BELOW: Down on the floor the air was much cleaner, where RS-3m 506 and an unidentified sister waited for service.
Colonie, NY, April 1986

ABOVE: Early morning sunlight is knifing through the thick fog that has rolled off of the Hudson River just a couple hundred yards away. It makes a great atmosphere in which to shoot Albany Port Railroad 1, an Alco S-2. Both of the red Alcos were former D&H locomotives.
Albany, NY, June 1979

OPPOSITE TOP: About eight miles south of the Colonie shops, two more Alcos could be found during the 1980's at the Port of Albany. Pictured here is Albany Port Railroad RS-3 2.
Albany, NY, April 1988

OPPOSITE BOTTOM: By 1992, both of the former Delaware & Hudson Alcos were in storage, replaced by two former Conrail SW-9's, 12 and 13. Here, No.12 shows off the new Albany Port Railroad paint scheme.
Albany, NY, May 1992

Selkirk Yard, Selkirk, NY

Built by the New York Central Railroad, Selkirk Yard opened in 1924. It covers approximately 632 acres, is six miles long, and almost one mile wide. The entire yard was reconstructed in 1968 by Penn Central. Today it is primarily configured as a classification yard, containing 70 tracks, with a 3,640-car capacity. The second largest section is the receiving yard's eleven tracks, which can accommodate 1,720 cars.

Security, post–911, is tight, but railfans gather almost daily at the Old School Road bridge that spans the yard, very conveniently intersecting the engine house and the fuel rack, as well as the approach to the hump yard. The railroad accepts the fans on the highway overpass, where some interesting photographs can be made.

ABOVE: I have made many trips to Selkirk Yard since my first January 1981 tour, and have been quite satisfied with photographing from the "Railfan Bridge". This view illustrates the amount of power serviced at the facility, which this day included visitors from the Housatonic Railroad and the New York, Susquehanna & Western. Selkirk, NY, July 1995

ABOVE: A two-year-old GE C40-8W leads a train of predominantly boxcar traffic into Selkirk Yard from the west. This is one of the views still available from the Old School Road "Railfan Bridge".   Selkirk, NY, May 1992

BELOW: This shot was made from the Route 9W overpass. Conrail SD40-2 6446 has a long string of revenue cars in tow as it starts its run down the River Line.   Selkirk, NY, December 1984

LEFT: Selkirk Yard has lost none of its intrigue under CSX ownership, as witnessed in this hump yard shot made from the railfan bridge.

Selkirk, NY, May 2000

BELOW: When my host at Conrail explained the "ground rules" for my visit, he cautioned me very sternly about entering the culvert when it was occupied, or about to be occupied, by a locomotive. Rail traffic and vehicular traffic share the culvert to get to the "inside" of the yard. Now I ask you, "Do you think someone needs to be told twice about that?" Going through the culvert, I was like a nine-year-old jumping off the diving board for the first time. I checked, then double-checked and then checked again, and like that nine year old, was very proud of myself when I got to the other side. That is the hump tower over the culvert.

Selkirk, NY, January 1981

ABOVE: Conrail SD-40s 6244 and 6332 have the James E. Strates carnival train in tow as they head out onto the one-mile-long Alfred H. Smith Memorial Bridge that crosses the Hudson River parallel to the Interstate I-90 span.   Coeymans, NY, June 1988

BELOW: A Chessie caboose brings up the markers on CIR-111, the James E. Strates train.   Coeymans, NY, June 1988

The West Shore — Selkirk to Newburgh

The area just south of Selkirk on the west shore of the Hudson River is known for its cement plants. The three major plants in the 32 miles between Selkirk and Cementon all contribute to River Line traffic. Only one, Holcim, still receives coal by rail, so outbound covered hoppers of cement account for 90% of the traffic generated by the industry. Farther south, the River Line runs through farmland and then crosses three different streams on very impressive trestles, as you will see in the following pages. At Catskill the line runs over the Catskill Creek on a high trestle. Farther south the River Line crosses Esopus Creek at Glenerie Falls, and finally at Wilbur, two miles south of the Kingston city limits, Rondout Creek is spanned by the very impressive Wilbur Trestle. At Newburgh we find one of the very few branch lines off the River Line. The Newburgh Industrial Track is a five-mile spur to Vails Gate, NY, that swings off of the main line then crosses above it on a curved trestle.

ABOVE: A pair of Conrail B23-7's get the "green board" they were waiting for and accelerate out of the siding at MP 106 in Alsen, NY. By climbing the embankment above Route 9W, the river can be pulled into this photo.   Alsen, NY, October 1995

OPPOSITE TOP: Three Chicago & North Western GP-50's team up with a lone Conrail locomotive to lead a westbound stack train at Ravena, NY. The train is about a half hour away from entering Selkirk Yard.   Ravena, NY, December 1990

OPPOSITE BOTTOM: That James E. Strates CIR-111 that we saw earlier crossing the Hudson on the Alfred H. Smith Bridge is seen here high above Catskill Creek. I was standing on a pedestrian footbridge in Catskill, NY, when I took this photo. The present-day footbridge was once a railroad bridge carrying the tracks of the Catskill Mountain Railroad.   Catskill, NY, June 1988

ABOVE: A CSX C44-9W and a C40-8 have an autorack unit train southbound across Catskill Trestle in Catskill, NY.

Catskill, NY, June 2005

BELOW: Two CSX AC44CW's are seen crossing the Catskill Creek Trestle as the hot box detector positioned just south of the trestle sings out "Conrail, Catskill, New York. No defects." Catskill, NY, June 2005

ABOVE: I positioned myself to the north side of Rondout Creek to capture this southbound Conrail stack train negotiating Wilbur Trestle in Kingston, NY.   Kingston, NY, July 1988

BELOW: Northbound (westbound by timetable) TV-53 races across the Glenerie Falls Trestle, above the rushing water of Esopus Creek. Sadly, this is one of those great shots that cannot be duplicated today. Residential development makes it difficult to get down to the falls, and if you can, you will find that the trees in the middle of the Esopus have grown up to block the view.   Glenerie, NY, June 1987

ABOVE: On their journey from Selkirk Yard to New Jersey, CSX River Subdivision trains cross some impressive bridges and trestles. This span at Esopus, NY, is not one of them. Q-154 heads up a southbound stack train.   Esopus, NY, May 2007

OPPOSITE TOP: CSX ES44-AC 703 has a stack train south through West Park. A new passing siding was constructed here in 2006 and the signal gantry was updated. Three different rural roads merge at a grade crossing here, providing a lot of visual interaction between the train and the crossing gates and flashing lights. It's a wonderful place to photograph CSX trains.   West Park, NY, May 2007

OPPOSITE BOTTOM: The ill-fated New Haven Railroad Poughkeepsie Bridge spanning the Hudson River looms over this empty unit coal train as it makes its way north through Highland, NY, to Selkirk. The bridge that once connected Hopewell Jct. on the east side of the river, to Maybrook Yard on the west side, caught fire during Penn Central ownership, resulting in the abandonment of that line. There is an effort underway to develop the enormous structure into a "linear park" which would offer spectacular photographic opportunities on both banks of the river— if you are willing to brave the 212 foot height above the river.   Highland, NY, July 1988

The West Shore — Newburgh to New Jersey

The area of the Hudson River Valley that we are now entering is one of the most scenic areas of the United States east of the Mississippi River. The natural beauty of the terrain, coupled with the fact that there is little industry along the west bank of the river, makes this area one that is sought out by naturalists, wildlife photographers and railfans alike. Our good fortune of few industries along the river is due in great part to the Palisades Park Commission, which in 1900 purchased almost all of the riverfront property in an area of the valley from the George Washington Bridge in Fort Lee, New Jersey, to the Bear Mountain Bridge in Fort Montgomery, New York. The formation of the Park Commission and the subsequent acquisition of the riverfront property was in response to several quarrying operations that had started to blast away at the world-famous Palisades, a formation of an igneous rock known as basalt. Thus, a large area with Revolutionary War history and natural beauty known as the Palisades has been preserved for us to share today. Enjoy it with me on the following pages.

ABOVE: Conrail's KI-70 was a local based out of Kingston, NY. It is pictured here ascending the trestle that will lift it up and over the River Line, which can be seen in the foreground, and onto the Newburgh Industrial Track, a vestage of the Erie Railroad's Newburgh Branch.
Newburgh, NY, April 1987

ABOVE: Conrail GP-38 7886 is on the Newburgh Industrial Track, crossing above the River Line. Looking down the main, a cut of cars left behind on the siding by the crew can be seen.
Newburgh, NY, March 1990

BELOW: Big CSX GE's, AC6000CW 5003 and AC4400CW 78, meet at CP-55 in Newburgh. The 5003 will wait for two southbound trains to pass before being cleared to continue north.
Newburgh, NY, April 2001

ABOVE: A very rare treat on the west shore of the Hudson— A special event at the West Point Military Academy commanded a chartered Amtrak train on the River Line. After its passengers detrained at West Point, the special ran north to Newburgh, where the power ran around its train for the return trip. The special is seen on the Newburgh siding while a Conrail general merchandise train passes.

Newburgh, NY, May 1987

BELOW: This photograph was made from the dock of West Point Military Academy. The Conrail southbound has some special loads on the head end as it passes the historic stone station made famous in the 1950's movie "The Long Gray Line" and later, a TV program of the same name.

West Point, NY, June 1993

ABOVE: I liked the previous shot so much I went back to the same location that weekend. Absent the cars in the parking lot, the photo location became even more appealing. Then, to really add excitement, a Conrail stack train arrived, led by foreign power in the form of Cotton Belt and CSX. It doesn't get much better than that!

West Point, NY, June 1993

BELOW: Still reveling in the euphoria of the Mets' World Series win, I decided it was time to become a railfan again. I took my cameras up to West Point and arrived in time to catch a northbound Conrail general merchandise train about to enter the short tunnel under one of the buildings. Regrettably, railfan photography at West Point is off limits post-911.

West Point, NY, October 1986

LEFT: This photo was made on one of those days in February when the temperature shoots up to the high 50's for a day or two in the northeast, just to tantalize you, before the mercury drops to sub-freezing again for another month and a half of winter. I took the opportunity to make a long and arduous hike into the woods for a very seldom seen view. Looking back at Storm King Mountain, you can see the precipice from which the shot below was taken. The island in the middle of the river is Bannermans, a landmark that is usually worked into shots from the east bank of the river.

Cornwall, NY, February 1991

ABOVE: Northbound Conrail TOFC train TV-24 stretches for a mile snaking along the Hudson. This shot was taken from Route 218 on Storm King Mountain.

Cornwall, NY, October 1986

26

ABOVE: South of West Point you will encounter a lot of nature photographers, especially bird watchers. Iona Island, farther south, is in fact a bird sanctuary and nesting site for the Bald Eagle. This winged show-off must have misinterpreted the reason for my camera!
Highland Falls, NY, December 1989

BELOW: It's nice when they show up well dressed! A pair of spotless SD-60's have a TOFC train in tow southbound on a wonderfully warm March afternoon. The ice in the river has melted, and spring buds are not far off. The large hill on the other side of the river is the 760-foot high Sugarloaf Hill.
Highland Falls, NY, March 1997

ABOVE: The ruggedness of the background in this shot is deceiving, as the photo is only about a half mile in from the roadway. This location is now double-tracked, as CSX has added a long siding here. Conrail B36-7 5051 was transferred to Norfolk Southern in 1999.
Ft. Montgomery, NY, March 1990

OPPOSITE TOP: Conrail B23-7 2022 is southbound approaching Ft. Montgomery with a track geometry train. The lineside poles that at times were a hindrance to photography, were also a great prop at other times, adding balance to the photo.   Highland Falls, NY, October 1986

OPPOSITE BOTTOM: A Conrail autorack train from the GM plant in Linden, NJ, is northbound on the banks of the river. I was one of several railfan photographers who would carry pruning shears in my camera bag to keep those bushes trimmed.
Highland Falls, NY, June 1990

ABOVE: It's early April, and the water in the river is still quite cold, but the kayakers from West Point Military Academy can't help but divert their attention from paddling to watch the long freight train. That's a pair of SD-50's on the point of the southbound.

Highland Falls, NY, April 1990

BELOW: TV-53 northbound through the Fort Montgomery Tunnel was usually the first train with enough daylight to photograph. The "53" stretches out for more than a mile in this shot taken from the walkway of the Bear Mountain Bridge.   Fort Montgomery, NY, October 1986

ABOVE: CSX train Q111 is led by C40-8 7523 as it exits the north portal of Fort Montgomery tunnel in early morning light.

Fort Montgomery, NY, April 2002

BELOW: GP40-2 3395 leads Conrail's hot shot TOFC train, TVLA, northbound out of the tunnel at Fort Montgomery.

Fort Montgomery, NY, March 1990

Fort Montgomery, Fort Clinton, Anthony's Nose, Bear Mountain and a whole bunch of "what ifs ?"

I think it is appropriate at this point to delve into a little history and some local legend regarding railroads and amusement parks never built, iron mines, and a major bridge spanning the Hudson River, designed for horse drawn wagons and railroad trains. All of the above have some factual foundation, some more substantial than others, however.

There were many small iron mines in the 1800's throughout the Ramapo Mountain chain, which is part of the Appalachian Mountains. The iron mines, and a desire for a shorter distance to transport Pennsylvania coal destined for New York City and major cities in Connecticut and Massachusetts, were the impetus for several railroads that went well beyond the planning stages, to financing and surveying of possible routes. The key to the successful completion of the new railroads would be the building of one or more suspension bridges over the Hudson River south of Poughkeepsie. One of these endeavors was named the Hudson River Suspension Bridge & New England Railway. The proposed route would take it from a connection with the Erie RR at Newburgh Junction (where the Harriman Metro North station stands today), over the Ramapo Mountains in Orange and Rockland Counties, over Bear Mountain and Dunderberg Mountain, and then over a suspension bridge strung from Fort Clinton (Fort Montgomery) on the west shore, to Anthony's Nose on the east shore. No less than Andrew Carnegie was involved in the project. Now for the penumbra where fact and lore blur. To examine the proposed route, it becomes apparent that the eastward route of the railroad would have taken a dramatic turn south at Bear Mountain, and then in a horseshoe curve that would have rivaled that of Altoona, PA, would have looped around Dunderberg Mountain and continued back north to Fort Clinton (now Fort Montgomery) and across the Hudson River on a suspension bridge that would have been built in the exact location of today's Bear Mountain Bridge. Lore has it that the reason for the loop was an amusement park and large hotel that was to be built atop Dunderberg Mountain overlooking Jones Point.

Standing on Iona Island and looking south along the ridge of Dunderberg, one can plainly see the right of way that had been built. A local historian named Bob (more about him later) told me he hiked to the top three different times and he reported that there is some track that can be found, as well as the bore of a tunnel that was started but never completed.

After the proposed New England Railway crossed the Hudson River at Anthony's Nose, plans were for it to interchange with the New York, Boston & Montreal Railroad– which was never built– at a location about twenty miles east of the bridge. More local legend says that footings were constructed on either side of the river for the new suspension bridge, and when the entire project was abandoned, the footings were used for the construction of the present bridge, which was built by E.H. Harriman, who controlled the Union Pacific and many other western railroads in the 1800's. Some fact and some legend surrounds the Harriman family and their impact on the area known today as Bear Mountain State Park and Harriman State Park. It seems that E.H. Harriman's wife, Mary Averell Harriman, became one of the nation's first NIMBY's when, in 1907, plans surfaced for a large state prison to be built at

ABOVE: CSX train Q-109 is southbound on a January morning when neither man nor beast should have been outside, let alone standing where the water and ice of the river are lapping at your waterproof boots.   Fort Montgomery, NY, January 2008

Bear Mountain. The Harriman family owned 30,000 acres between the Hudson River at Fort Montgomery, and Arden, NY, on Route 17 to the west. A prison next to their property just wouldn't do. When her husband, E.H. Harriman, died the following year, Mrs. Harriman made a proposal to the Governor of New York. She would donate one-third of the Harriman Estate, 10,000 acres, and $1,000,000 to establish Bear Mountain State Park, and put an end to any talk about a prison. Her adult son, William Averell Harriman, actually presented the deed and $1,000,000 check to the governor in 1909. Sometime later, William Averell Harriman himself would become the 48th Governor of New York . When Bear Mountain State Park was established, most of the iron mines were shut down. The town of Baileytown, which supported one of the largest mines, disappeared from the map.

Remember the elderly local historian Bob, the intrepid climber? Bob had another great story of riding his bicycle with several friends to the iron mine at Baileytown long after it closed. When that mine had been active, the iron ore would travel in iron buckets suspended on a pulley system about twelve miles long. The pulley system ended on the Hudson River, near the rock cut just north of the Fort Montgomery Tunnel, where the ore would be dumped into barges to be towed to foundries along the river. The boys would get into one of the buckets, and with a great shove from a friend, could travel a mile or two. On one day in particular, it was Bob's turn in the bucket. His friends gave him a push and then rode off on their bicycles to meet him farther down the line. Well, it seems that the shove was not hardy enough, and after only a half mile or so, the bucket came to a stop, right in the middle of a lake that the system crossed. Bob, did his best to get the bucket moving again, all to no avail. Finally, as afternoon became evening, he gave into the inevitable and jumped from the bucket into the lake. After swimming ashore he met up with his comrades who had come back looking for him.

OPPOSITE TOP: Traffic is light this morning on the Bear Mountain Bridge. I have made the climb half way up the mountain known as Anthony's Nose to photograph this Conrail southbound. The east side of the bridge is anchored to the mountain. There is a marked trail leading hikers up the mountain, but it's not an easy climb. Open-heart surgery a few years later would curtail any more adventures on Anthony's Nose, so I'm glad I made the climb several times when I still could. There is a message here– Don't put it off– go and do it– and enjoy every minute of it, whatever "it" is.

Fort Montgomery, NY, October 1996

OPPOSITE BOTTOM: SD-40 6292 leads a nice selection of power north across the Fort Montgomery trestle on a hazy July morning. Fort Montgomery, NY, July 1983

ABOVE: C40-8W 6124 leads an autorack unit train south out of the tunnel and across the Fort Montgomery trestle on a very warm June morning. It was a good day to stay close to the water. Fort Montgomery, NY, June 1993

ABOVE: I made the climb almost to the top of the mountain for this shot. High above the stanchions of the bridge, I captured a southbound Conrail TOFC train. Above the River Line, in that clump of trees to the left of the bridge, are bears, snakes, eagles and wolves, better known as the Bear Mountain Zoo. It was from this mountain, known as Anthony's Nose, that General George Clinton stretched an iron chain across the Hudson River to Fort Montgomery in an attempt to prevent the British fleet from sailing up the river.

Fort Montgomery, NY, August 1995

ABOVE: From the Route 9W bridge we witness the passing of a northbound Conrail general merchandise train as it traverses Popolopen Creek. Across the river we can look right through "Middle Tunnel" on the Metro North Hudson Line.   Fort Montgomery, NY, January 1985

BELOW: Sixteen years after the above photograph was made, a pair of CSX EMD's have a southbound train on the Fort Montgomery Trestle. The trees in the foreground are showing just a hint of turning foliage.   Fort Montgomery, NY, September 2001

OPPOSITE TOP: Contrary to first appearance, there is no climbing involved in this shot; just park the car and shoot from the east side of the Bear Mountain Bridge. That's CSX train Q-109 southbound in glorious fall foliage.   Fort Montgomery, NY, November 1999

OPPOSITE BOTTOM: You don't need to have great fall foliage to make a nice photo in the lower Hudson Valley, and you don't have to put your camera away for the winter either. A CSX stack train starts across Popolopen Creek in the dead of winter. If you look closely at this photo you will see, just behind the train, the then-new construction of a footbridge that spanned the creek during the Revolutionary War.   Fort Montgomery, NY, February 2003

37

ABOVE: This is a day I soon won't forget. The weatherman was calling for light snow, and I figured I could get over to Bear Mountain for some snow shots. What the weather turned out to be was freezing sleet that made driving (and walking back to the car) impossible. I finally did get back to the car and realized that I could not go anywhere because of the icy roads. I sat in the car for several hours listening to occasional horrific-sounding automobile crashes of motorists who were foolish enough to attempt to drive. After a couple of hours the "Low Fuel" warning light came on, so I was forced to turn off the engine and sit in the cold. After the state DOT sander passed for a second time I mustered enough courage to get to the nearest gas station for fuel and a hot coffee. I love this shot of SD40-2 6471 passing the long-since-removed target signal at MP 41, but I paid dearly for it ! Bear Mountain, NY, February 1992

OPPOSITE TOP: One of the attributes of railfanning the River Line is, in most instances, you can get a great scenic shot in either direction and on either side of the track. I submit this shot taken on a warm summer morning at MP 41, where SD40-2 6447 has charge of a southbound autorack train. Bear Mountain, NY, August 1991

OPPOSITE BOTTOM: The Hudson River, for all of its beauty, can turn angry and mean at times. Four consecutive days of heavy rain, coupled with a lunar high tide, has pushed the river right to the edge of Conrail's right-of-way. Bear Mountain Landing Park, a fisherman's favorite, will be flooded by the end of the day. The amount of debris in the water is testimony to the ferocity of the storms. The northbound Conrail train is operating under slow orders as a precautionary measure. Fort Montgomery, NY, April 1987

ABOVE: I am a big advocate of exploring different angles and views at a single location. Just because the photo doesn't look good from one angle, don't walk away, it may look good from another perspective by simply changing your location. Train SEOI (Selkirk, NY, to Oak Island, Newark, NJ) is seen passing MP-41, photographed by climbing the rocks on the west side of the tracks.

Bear Mountain, NY, October 1989

ABOVE: This is a view looking through Ring Meadow. This day I found a hill to climb, and once up the hill, a tree to climb as well. My efforts on this crystal clear March day were rewarded with a southbound SEOI and a unique view of the curvature of Conrail's tracks looking south. In the river, partially obscured by a branch, one tugboat is shoving a barge of gasoline north, closely followed by a second tug. Across the river is the City of Peekskill and Peekskill Bay, still jammed with ice.   Iona Island, NY, March 1994

Iona Island

An Introduction and History

There is no single section of the Hudson River Valley, on either side of the river, as well known and important to the railfan community as Iona Island. That is saying a lot, considering the overall beauty of the river and the distance we are covering from Colonie to New York City. However, Iona Island, in approximately two-and-a-half miles, offers more photographic opportunities than any other stretch of the Hudson River Valley. It has become a meeting place for railfans from several different states. Some fans drive in and sit in their cars waiting for the trains. Others hike along the rail line to any of the twenty or so popular photographic locations. The most intrepid not only hike, but climb rocks and hills in search of new vistas.

Not everyone carrying a camera at Iona Island is a railfan. The 129 acres are a wildlife preserve, and in particular, a bird sanctuary to migratory birds in the summer and bald eagles during the winter months.

Iona Island at one time was actually two different islands; Salisbury and the much smaller Round Island. The two were joined by a landfill project of the United States Navy in the early 20th Century. The history of the island dates back to 1849, when the two islands and the surrounding tidal flat marshes known as Salisbury and Ring meadows were purchased by John Beveridge. He then leased a large portion of the tract to his son-in-law, who planned on growing grapes and establishing a winery on the island. However, that business failed and the property was developed as a spa and retreat. A large hotel was erected on the property, known as the Mountain House. A railroad station, Ferris wheel and picnic grounds were soon added. Heavyweight boxing champ John L. Sullivan trained there at times. The Navy purchased the islands in 1899 and constructed an ordnance depot for the assembly and storage of ammunition and large shells during World War I. The complex was expanded during World War II, and at the height of the war there were as many as 50 buildings on the grounds. At the south end of the main gate, tracks leading into the complex can still be found. A 35- ton Whitcomb was stationed inside the ordnance depot by the U.S. Navy to switch cars in the complex. It had been purchased new by the Navy in 1937 and was sold in 1947 to Fruit Growers Express of Alexandria, Virginia, when Iona Island Ordnance Depot was decommissioned.

In July 1927 there was a train accident at Iona Island which claimed the lives of four passengers on a New York, Ontario & Western train that had originated in Summitville in Sullivan County, northwest of the River Line. The NYO&W passenger train left its home rails at Cornwall Landing for the last leg of its journey to Weehawken, NJ, on the tracks of the New York Central's West Shore Railroad (now CSX's River Subdivision). The NYO&W had trackage rights over the West Shore Railroad from Cornwall to Weehawken. At about 11:30 AM on July 5, 1927, NYO&W train 124, with Mother Hubbard-type steam engine 246 on the point, was crowded with vacationers returning to the City when it crossed the Iona Island trestle at Bear Mountain. At the same time, a New York Central way-freight that carried unoccupied passenger cars on its rear was negotiating the switches at the Iona Island NYC passenger station, moving from the eastbound main to a siding in between the two mains. The movement was controlled by automatic block signals in the form of two semaphores. While the unoccupied passenger cars of the wayfreight still fouled the eastbound main, the speeding NYO&W train ran a signal at the east end of Iona Trestle (as per the ICC investigation dated August 4, 1927) and rear-ended the train entering the siding. The impact of the collision separated the body of a baggage car, the first car of the train behind #246's tender, and telescoped the car body over and through the first coach, killing three passengers instantly, with one more perishing a short time later at the West Point Military Infirmary. Twenty-three other passengers were injured.

Today the Naval Depot, railroad station, sidings, semaphore signals and both railroads involved in the accident are long since history. The CSX single track at milepost 41 offers no hint of the above events when railfan photographers gather at Iona Island to delight in the scenery and the opportunity to meet and chat with other fans.

ABOVE: CSX C40-8 7518 leads a TOFC train south over the Iona Trestle on a sunny but bitterly cold January day. The lack of ice in the river indicates that this may have been the first severely cold weather in some time. As far as the photographer was concerned, the sun illuminating the train wasn't giving off much warmth.   Iona Island, NY, January 2001

BELOW: CSX SD-60 8717, still dressed in Conrail blue, is followed by Helm Leasing SD40-2 8166 and at least one NS GP15-1, providing a pretty wild consist southbound through Iona   Iona Island, NY, September 2000

ABOVE: A pair of spotless eleven-year-old SD50's, with a little help from a somewhat older SD40-2, has one of the longest trains I have ever witnessed on the River Line moving along briskly. The train stretches out over the Iona Island Trestle, the Fort Montgomery Trestle and into the Fort Montgomery Tunnel! Iona Island, NY, February 1995

BELOW: Conrail SD40-2 6481 leads a northbound autorack train over the wooden Iona Island Trestle before it was rebuilt with steel. Notice the open-top autorack cars, normal for the era. The second locomotive in the consist, SD-40 6357, is a former Pennsylvania RR unit soon to be traded in to EMD and join its lease fleet. Iona Island, NY, April 1983

OPPOSITE TOP: Foreign, or "run through," power is always a treat on the River Line. What could be more interesting than a lashup of C&NW SD-60 8046, UP C40-8 9298 and UP SD-60 6080 on a Conrail double stack train? Iona Island, NY, September 1991

OPPOSITE BOTTOM: CSX SD40-2 8811 has recently-retired Burlington Northern (now HLCX) C30-7 5030 tucked in as the second unit on this southbound through Iona Island. Iona Island, NY, August 2000

45

ABOVE: It's a dreary day in late March as Conrail train OCS (Office Car Special) negotiates the Iona Island trestle with its train of heavy-weight passenger cars. This view is testimony to the once double-track on the old wooden trestle.   Iona Island, NY, March 1983

BELOW: The new steel trestle at Iona Island is in service as C40-8 6035 and SD-50 6721 power a northbound OISE. The majority of the train is still box cars.   Iona Island, NY. February 1992

ABOVE: Conrail is just a little more than two years old, and most of its motive power has yet to be repainted into the new blue scheme. Thankfully, on this day, the good fellow who put this train together stuck GP40-2 3307 on the point. The trailing units are a GP40, a GP38-2 with the smallest CR markings I have ever seen, and a GP38-2 still with no CR markings at all. That's Route 6/ 202 cut into the mountainside on the other side of the river.
Iona Island, NY, December 1978

BELOW: Standing below the trestle on the shore line gives a different perspective on the construction of the new steel trestle. The wooden span was left in place while the steel structure was built on the inland side. A pair of C40-8 widecabs leads a nice lashup of power on this mid-morning Q-111.
Iona Island, NY, July 1999

ABOVE: I had to include this shot in order to tell the story of the seagulls of the Iona Island Trestle. For years now, a flock of seagulls has been roosting on the inland handrail of the trestle, and to watch this play out, you have to think that they are playing chicken with the passing trains. As a train approaches, a couple might flap their wings, but they sit tight. When the train is really close, one or two of the less-daring birds flee, but the rest wait for the train to be almost next to them before they all take off right in front of the lead locomotive. Sebastian Seagull here, waited the longest I have ever seen and got blasted with the hot exhaust of a pair of AC6000CW's for his bravery.

Iona Island, NY, August 2001

BELOW: Conrail train SEEN (Selkirk, NY, to Enola, PA), led by C30-7A 6535, has crossed the Iona Island trestle southbound and is about to duck through a rock cut. Earlier, I lamented that a number of the photos in this book are no longer available for a variety of reasons, including the growth of vegetation. This is one of those instances where vegetation obscures 90% of the train from this vantage point today.

Iona Island, NY, April 1990

ABOVE: A couple of very rare visitors— Burlington Northern SD-70 MAC's lead CSX train Q-254 southbound through Iona. One might refer to them as Black & Tan (I'll hoist a pint to that, Lad) or black & gold, in which case I should have photographed them at West Point; black and gold being the cadet's team colors (Beat Navy, oooh haa!!!)   Iona Island, NY, April 2001

BELOW: A pair of AC6000CW's lead Q-409 through Iona Island and past the site of the 1927 accident. On this day there were three large Bald Eagles flying around the island, giving a couple of railfans a treat in between trains.   Iona Island, NY, January 2002

ABOVE: A couple showed up, and after a long walk along the right-of-way, found this secluded spot and spread out their blanket on the edge of Doodletown Bight to sunbathe far away from the maddening crowds. Then four guys showed up with crab nets to crab from the trestle. Then a southbound Conrail train showed up with four giant-blue locomotives blowing the horn at the four crabbers who were too close to the tracks. Perhaps the young lady was saying to her boyfriend "Why don't we just set up our blanket in the middle of Times Square?"

Iona Island, NY, May 1988

BELOW: Don't settle for one spot, or one angle. Search out every possible angle for each shot. As TV-400 progresses south, led by a pair of SD-50's, to the left of the left-hand number board is a small spit of rock on the hill in the distance, from where the above photograph was taken. It's a tough hike up to that location but if you get up there watch where you sit, there is a lot of cactus up there. Cactus in New York State? I dug up some on a subsequent trip and replanted it in my backyard. It produces a beautiful large yellow flower in early summer.

Iona Island, NY, July 1987

ABOVE: Sometimes you have to do a lot of hiking and exploring to find a new photographic angle. However, when you do find a shot like this, it's all worth it. Doodletown Bight is comprised of tidal shallows and mud flats. (For those of you not up on old English, a bight is a small bay in a river). The stream in the foreground is Doodletown Creek, which runs through Ring Meadow and under the small wooden trestle and into the Hudson River. It starts about two and a half miles west, high on Bear Mountain where the hamlet of Doodletown once stood, and cascades down to river level. Iona Island, NY, April 1987

BELOW: Sometimes, not often, the Hudson River becomes as still as a lake. This was one of those times and I am glad I was there to make this photograph of CSX SD40-2 and some leased units powering Q-402 north. Iona Island, NY. July 2000

ABOVE: A southbound Conrail OCS (Office Car Special), and this one was really special. The first half of the train was comprised of Conrail's cars, while the rear was Chicago & North Western's attractively painted business train. The rain had held off all morning, and didn't start until the very end of the train was passing. How is that for good timing?   Iona Island, NY, August 1987

BELOW: The Ringling Brothers and Barnum & Bailey Circus "Red Unit" is crossing Doodletown Creek behind B23-7's 1958 and 1960. That certainly is the location to photograph a long and impressive train.   Iona Island, NY, May 1990

OPPOSITE: SD80MAC 4102 is less than a year old and looking great in this shot from the south end of the island. The bend of the branches follow the curvature of Bear Mountain. Great planning ? Nah, I didn't even notice it until I got the slide back from Kodak.
                Iona Island, NY, September 1996

ABOVE: Those bruises on my backside are self-inflicted. After finding this view (from Route 9-W) I shot two southbounds that afternoon and vowed to return soon. Soon was not soon enough. I forgot about the location for almost two years, during which time trees grew and filled in the small hole through which this photo was taken. The trees are down an incredibly steep embankment, so there is no way to reach them to climb and no way to trim them. The only thing left to do is kick yourself, and well, trust me, that has been done.

Iona Island, NY, June 1991

BELOW: This is a location that required some climbing, but the view of the river and the City of Peekskill on the other shore made the effort worth it. The barren trees in the foreground have grown since, and now obscure much of this shot. That's KI-70, the local from Kingston, NY, returning home after working as far south as Stony Point.

Milepost 40, south of Iona Island, NY, March 1990

The River Line

Stony Point, NY, to Oak Island (Newark, NJ)

After passing through the Haverstraw Tunnel bored under Route 9-W, which has shadowed the River Line from all the way from Selkirk Yard, the track begins to head inland, putting distance between the railroad and the Hudson River. The River Line, now CSX's River Subdivision, intersects the towns of West Nyack, Orangeburg and Tappan, New York, and then Northvale, Bogota and West Englewood, New Jersey, before ultimately ending at Oak Island Yard in Newark, NJ, on the outskirts of Newark's Liberty Airport. It has extended 132.6 miles from Selkirk Yard, traveling through one of the most beautiful river valleys in the world.

ABOVE: A pair of SD-50's lead a southbound train past the audible Stony Point hot box and dragging equipment detector, which is out of view to the right in this photo. After World War II, dozens of Merchant Marine "Liberty Ships" were moored in this cove as part of the National Defense Reserve Fleet. Their holds were loaded with surplus grain, because the United States agricultural industry was still producing crops as if it were wartime. It seemed like a good idea at the time, a great place to store surplus grain and utilize the decommissioned ships. Rats soon discovered that they could swim from shore and climb the anchor chains. Their reward would be all the grain they could eat. Soon all of the grain was contaminated, and the Tompkins Cove section of Stony Point was overrun with very large water rats. Today, a pair of anchors mark the former site of the "Liberty Ships". A bronze tablet in a stone monument tells the story of the fleet, but conveniently leaves out the story about the rodents.
Stony Point, NY, March 1994

ABOVE: CSX 7867 leads a hotshot TOFC train south at Haverstraw, NY. The track at right is the lead into the Mirant Power Plant. One of Mirant's SW-8's will soon come out of the plant to pick up a cut of hoppers to feed the coal fired furnaces.

Haverstraw, NY, February 2006

BELOW: CSX local C-712 has Mirant Power SW-8 #1 in tow on October 9, 2008, as the switcher rolls over its home rails for the last time. The EMD, built in 1952, was sold to LTE in Mc Donald, Ohio, to be scrapped or cannibalized as a parts source for other EMD switchers. On November 25, 2008, the lower Hudson River Valley shook as the plant's 475-foot tall smokestack was toppled using 100 pounds of dynamite.

Haverstraw, NY, October 2008

RIGHT: This is an example of a CSX train flying our flag after 911. In this view, the unit autorack train occupies the main, southbound at CP-35, the beginning of a 9,234 foot-long siding. This photograph was made by hacking my way east through briar bushes and vines from the Revolutionary War Stony Point Battlefield.

Stony Point, NY, October 2001

BELOW: On a cold January day, C39-8 6004 is cresting the grade at CP-35. The plow on the big GE gives an indication that it has been battling snow for most of the trip south from Selkirk.

Stony Point, NY, January 1998

ABOVE: TOFC train Q-111, led by a pair of AC 6000CW's, is northbound on the siding through the Stoney Point Battlefield at Milepost 35.
Stony Point, NY, April 2002

BELOW: TV 24 is pictured northbound under the conveyor of the Tilcon-Tomasso rock quarry. The rear of the train is most likely still in the Haverstraw Tunnel. South of the tunnel, the line heads inland, and while still in the Hudson River Valley, the river is not visible.
Stony Point, NY, June 1986

ABOVE: A unique photo of an empty unit coal train southbound through Stony Point, high above the river. This location has since become obscured by trees. Several industries can be seen along the west shore of the river, starting with the Tilcon-Tomasso rock quarry in the foreground, then the twin stacks of the Bowline Plant of the Orange & Rockland Power Co. This facility is south of the now-closed O&R plant in Tompkins Cove that had received coal by rail and whose single stack is visible beyond the white structures of the US Gypsum plant.

Stony Point, NY, December 1988

BELOW: The Mayo Inn has changed little since the days of passenger service on the River Line. I could never determine if the baggage wagon was purchased to lend atmosphere, or if trains really stopped at the Inn. This location has changed dramatically, and the River Line is now fenced here, making this shot impossible today.

Congers, NY, November 1988

The Hudson Line: Rensselaer to Croton-Harmon

Passenger Service

Unlike the freight-only railroad on the west bank of the Hudson River, the passenger line on the east bank, known as the Hudson Line, has less contact with the banks of the river and therefore has a tendency to be somewhat bland from a photographic sense until it reaches Poughkeepsie. Trains leaving the Albany-Rensselaer station travel south behind a veil of trees and vegetation that for the most part hides the river. The line instead hugs the fringes of cities like Hudson and Rhinecliff, NY offering a view of the downtown areas but little else. However, when the Hudson Line reaches a point just south of Poughkeepsie the scenery jumps to life and rivals that of The River Line on the opposite shore.

ABOVE: Amtrak SW-1 742, built in July 1948 as Pennsylvania RR 9143, is in the process of switching a pair of F-40's at Amtrak's Rensselaer Shops. After several years of duty at Rensselaer, the SW-1 would be sent to work at Union Station in Washington, DC.
Rensselaer, NY, August 1982

ABOVE: A pair of spotless Amtrak FL-9's, 486 and 489, have train 48, the eastbound *Lake Shore Limited* into Albany-Rensselaer on time. Several cars from the rear of the train will be cut off to make the Boston section of the train, then #486 and 489 will continue into Grand Central Terminal in New York City.   Rensselaer, NY, July 1983

BELOW: Action at milepost 58 on the Hudson Line— Amtrak F-40 408 with a funky number board is in charge of northbound train 63, the *Maple Leaf*, while Conrail train NHSE (New Haven, CT, to Selkirk, NY, via the Maybrook Line) waits its turn on the branch. Large GE locomotives were assigned to these Maybrook Line freights, and this day a trio of C30-7's will ensure that NHSE will not cause any delays on the speedway known as the Hudson Line.   Beacon, NY, March 1990

ABOVE: Amtrak train 291 has just passed under the Selkirk Branch, which allows freight service on the Hudson Line access to and from Selkirk Yard via the A.H. Smith Memorial Bridge. The Selkirk Branch diverges from the Hudson Line at CP 125. Stuyvesant, NY, July 2008

BELOW: It is late in the day when train 235 rounds the curve approaching Rhinecliff station. The street lights in the parking lot have already been illuminated, and most of the pleasure boats on the Hudson River have returned to their marinas. Many of the passengers disembarking at Rhinecliff make the two-hour commute to New York City daily. Rhinecliff, NY, July 2008

ABOVE: Train 63, the *Maple Leaf,* slips under an abandoned through-truss bridge and past a modern set of signals as it approaches the station at Hudson, NY, on its northbound journey to Toronto.

Hudson, NY, July 2008

BELOW: Amtrak FL-9 489 has the *Lake Shore Limited* southbound (eastbound on the timetable) past the southern face of 1,260-foot high Breakneck Mountain. The Hudson Line's twin bores through the base of the mountain are just beyond the last car of the train.

Cold Spring, NY, April 1990

ABOVE: This is a view of Breakneck Mountain taken from Storm King Mountain on the west side of the river. That's Amtrak train making its way north along the Hudson on a very warm summer afternoon.
Cold Spring, NY, September 1986

OPPOSITE: I was able to capture an Amtrak Turboliner speeding past Breakneck Mountain and the Breakneck Lodge Restaurant, perched precariously at its base. I have to admit that I was quite uncomfortable the day I attended a wedding there. I imagine that monolith will stand unchanged for the next hundred years, but maybe not. I just wish there had not been so much bass in the music, it could have loosened some rock!
Cold Spring, NY, March 1990

ABOVE: Add some snow to Breakneck Mountain and let your imagination run wild. Is it the Rocky Mountains of Colorado or the Selkirk Mountains of Canada? The engineer and conductor in Metro North cab control car 6107 are no doubt enjoying the warm sun on a very frigid day. I wonder if the two of them are laughing at the freezing photographer. Thank goodness for tripods, I was shivering so much that a hand-held shot would have been just a blur.

Cold Spring, NY, January 1990

BELOW: Ahh, this is more like it! A beautiful and warm June day and the evening northbound rush has just started. The spit of land I have found for this photo is at the base of Mount Taurus, like Breakneck Mountain, it is part of the Appalachian chain. This section is separated from the main slope of Mount Taurus by Route 9-D and Metro North Railroad. As a photographer or hiker in this area, you have to be aware of (from largest to smallest) coyotes, red fox (many of which are rabid), eastern timber rattlesnakes and the tiniest threat: the deer tick, no larger than a grain of pepper, but can infect you with debilitating Lyme Disease. Putting all of that in perspective is a pair of FL-9's on the causeway, making the critters just an afterthought. High up on the hill is a large white building known as Dicks Castle.

Cold Spring, NY, June 1990

ABOVE: Passengers aboard Amtrak train 48, the *Lake Shore Limited,* are marveling at the scenery of the Hudson Highlands. Perhaps the most interesting is the ruins of Bannerman's Arsenal on Pollopel Island. Cold Spring, NY, May 1985

Bannerman's Island in the Hudson River at Cold Spring, and The Story of Dick's Castle at Garrison, NY

Probably the single object that railfans photographing the Hudson Line work into their photos more than any other, with the exception of the Bear Mountain Bridge, is Bannerman's Castle. Truly a castle in every sense of the word when it was constructed, the structures that make up the castle today are just empty and fire-gutted shells. Originally, there were seven buildings on the island, one elaborate residence and six buildings that comprised the largest private arsenal in the world. The design and much of the construction was the effort of Frank Bannerman, a Scotsman born in Dundee, Scotland, in 1851. His family emigrated to the U.S. when Frank was three years old. His father opened a business in Brooklyn, NY, selling used and surplus marine items, which after the Civil War morphed into surplus military items, including black gun powder. As the business grew, the Bannermans relocated to larger quarters several times. At the end of the Spanish American War, and with Frank at the helm, the company purchased 90 percent of all captured goods in a sealed bid. It then became necessary to find a secure place to store their large quantity of weapons and black powder. Frank's son David, saw Pollopel Island (pronounced Polly-pel) in the Hudson River, and Frank Bannerman purchased it in 1900. The island, which is six and three quarter acres of rock, is located about 1,000 feet from shore, about midway between Beacon and Cold Spring.

ABOVE: The ruins of Bannerman's Arsenal on Pollopel Island are viewed from the east shore of the Hudson River.

Cold Spring, NY, November 2008

At the time Bannerman purchased Pollopel Island to build his arsenal, it already had a long and rich military past. The very first settlers in the Cold Spring area took refuge on the island whenever they saw the beacon fires burning atop 1,530-foot Fishkill Mountain (later renamed Mount Beacon) to the north, indicating that Indians were on raiding parties. The Indians were superstitious and afraid of the island, and would not follow the settlers there. These signal fires worked so well that during the Revolutionary War, the Continental Army was warned of British troop movement by using beacon fires. The mountain on which the fires were lit is in the town that took its name from those fires; Beacon, NY. In 1902, the Otis Elevator Company of Yonkers, NY, opened an incline railway to the top of Mount Beacon which ascended a 65% grade, the steepest in the world at the time. An arson fire in 1983 burned all of the buildings on the mountain top and closed the incline railway.

Local Revolutionary War patriots used Pollopel Island from which to attack the British Fleet in the Hudson River. They also laced the river with upright logs sunk into the riverbed, tipped in steel. This was another attempt to stop the British fleet from sailing up the Hudson.

Frank Bannerman built his arsenal between 1901 to the time of his death in 1918. In August 1920, two years after his death, an explosion on the island damaged several of the storage buildings. By the 1950's, business had fallen off, and the Bannerman family moved most of the stored weaponry off the island, and they took up residence in New York City. Then, on August 8, 1969, an arson fire was ignited by vandals which completely destroyed the seven buildings that were still standing at that time. It is curious that most local accounts of that fire, especially those of very worthwhile organization attempting to save the ruins, fail to mention that the substantial explosions on the island at the time of the fire, deposited debris 1,020 feet away on the tracks of the then Penn Central Railroad. I had a trackside discussion with a former Penn Central employee who had been dispatched to clear the tracks. We can surmise from those accounts that some explosives had been left behind when the island was abandoned by the Bannermans. Today the island is owned by New York State which, in conjunction with The Bannerman Castle Trust, is attempting to restore portions of the island and castle and to eventually reopen the island for tours.

Dick's Castle

Many a railroad photographer has labored to work Dick's Castle into the background of a photograph, whether taken on the Hudson Line or from across the Hudson on the River Line.

In 1903 a very wealthy New York City financier named Evans P. Dick purchased 125 acres of land atop a large hill in Garrison, New York, directly across the Hudson River from the U.S. Military Academy at West Point. He began to build a large castle, following the design of one he had visited in Granada, Spain. Dick poured millions into the construction of the outer shell of the castle— the 45,000-square-foot structure was designed to include 25 fireplaces and more than 50 rooms, including an 86-foot-high tower. In 1911, with little more than the outer walls and a roof completed, the millionaire went bankrupt and abandoned further construction. The building and its 125-acre property languished for many years, falling into ruin. In 1944 a Slovak businessman from Yonkers, New York, came upon the property which reminded him of his Austrian-Hungarian birthplace. Anton Chmela, a tool and die maker, originally trained by Bell Labs, had struck out on his own at the outset of World War II, supplying the military with quartz crystals for radio transmitters and radar equipment. Chmela purchased the entire 125 acres and the dilapidated building. The structure that he purchased had very little interior detail; walls and floors had never been constructed. As the war drew to a close, Chmela moved his company, American Quartz Labs of Irvington, New York, to the basement of the castle, and began living in one of the many out-buildings that had been easier to make habitable. During the following 32 years, he continued construction of the large castle and moved in his extended family. Accounts of the children growing up in Dick's Castle— his own two children and numerous nieces and nephews— read like a Huck Finn novel, with a private waterfall and lake for swimming, private roads to learn to drive the family bulldozer, and acres of wild fruits to be picked by the children and canned by Mrs. Chmela. It is unclear why the Chmela family finally sold the still-unfinished building in 1979, but the deed was in fact transferred to a New York City art foundation that spent several hundred thousand completing the interior— and then decided not to use it. Again the building sat vacant, and it once again began to deteriorate until an wealthy real estate tycoon purchased the building in 1987 with hopes of turning it into a health spa or wedding reception complex. After only minor investment in repairs to the structure, other priorities forced him to sell it in 1989 to a group of developers who began investing in the structure. That group of investors soon went bankrupt, and the real estate tycoon returned to purchase the property for a second time. This time, in response to opposition to commercial development from neighbors, he divided a section of the castle into six condo apartments, some as large as 7,000 square feet. That is where Dick's Castle stands today, well over 100 years old with a still incomplete interior. It still makes an interesting backdrop for railfan photography, however.

ABOVE: I believe there is a story behind every photograph a railfan takes. It might only be a very short story, but I don't think photographers are out there, day-after-day, at the same locations photographing just to kill time. Here is the story behind this shot: There is a small road that leads down to the railroad and river. I had attempted to walk down the road a couple of times but some of the residents came out to "chase" me away, arguing that it is private property, although I knew it was not. Not wanting to make hard feelings, I left without arguing. After two failed attempts to get to what I believed would be a great location, I enlisted the aid of my wife and two young kids of a friend, as my kids were all in high school at the time. This time my wife and I walked down the road, each leading a small child by the hand. One of the residents came out to say "Hello!" The story doesn't end there, either. The two young girls loved seeing the trains so much that day, their mom had to eventually buy them a H.O. train set! As for the photo, that's #48 running on the "wrong" main, which really enhances the shot. The complex on the other side of the river is West Point.   Garrison, NY, July 1986

BELOW: This stone-arch bridge seemed a little out of place in 1989, as it does today. It is on private property, and so it has not been replaced by a utilitarian steel structure of some kind. A pair of FL-9's have #48 moving briskly this day.   Manitou, NY, April 1989

ABOVE: This and the following photo were taken the same day, about an hour apart. I risked life and limb on snowy roads to get there. Shooting in the snow is not easy, because your eye sees reflected light, but the camera does not. Many snow shots thus turn out dark and underexposed. Photographs of fast moving trains in the snow are even more difficult ! The SPV-2000's had a reputation of shutting down in blowing snow, but apparently not this day.   Manitou, NY, January 1988

BELOW: About an hour after the SPV-2000's went north, Amtrak FL-9 491 came blowing past milepost 46. That's the Bear Mountain Bridge in the background. The yellow apparatus on the ground are third-rail shoe rakes, which knock off improperly positioned third rail shoes. Although they have no function for a northbound train, southbound trains can operate on either track, hence two sets of rakes. Third rail territory begins about one mile north of Croton-Harmon, where southbound diesel trains have the option to operate on third rail current. The third rail pick up shoe, which is raised to a vertical position in diesel territory, must be lowered to the proper horizontal position before entering electrified territory. If the shoe does not position properly, it can cause damage to the third rail system, hence the rakes to knock off improperly seated shoes. That's not a good place to be standing if a shoe is knocked off at speed!   Manitou, NY, January 1988

ABOVE: 1988 was a year of extremes. It was as hot in the summer as it was snowy that winter. On this scorcher of an August morning, I found a northbound Amtrak turbo cutting through the heat and haze just north of the Bear Mountain Bridge. The turbos ran on an aircraft-type kerosene-fuel, and on this day the residue just stuck to your skin as the train passed, making it even more uncomfortable.

Manitou, NY, August 1988

ABOVE: At signal 46, track 1 is occupied by a pair of southbound SPV-2000s. The Beach Boy-looking fellow in the window is likely the Metro North conductor, taking an opportunity to observe the route.   Manitou, NY, November 1990

ABOVE: A Metro North FL-9 and an F-10 are northbound in the historic Hudson Valley. In the foreground is the remains of a Revolutionary War era kiln at the location where the "Great Chain" was forged and draped across the river to impede the British Fleet. More likely than not, this kiln had some significance in the forging of that chain.

Manitou, NY, March 1992

ABOVE: After the final rebuilding of the FL-9's, they were given the nickname "Starships" by shop personnel because of all their advanced electronics. The name became popular, and was picked up by the railfan community as well. A pair of "Starships" is pushing hard as they run along side a Hudson River estuary. The river itself is on the other side of the train.   Manitou, NY, November 1999

BELOW: Manitou was comprised a of spartan grade crossing and a diminutive flag stop "station" in the 1970's and 80's. The same small shelter still stands today, but is now smartly painted and landscaped. The grade crossing has also been upgraded to a modern rubberized version.   Manitou, NY, October 1980

ABOVE: It's fall in the Hudson River Valley, and the foliage show is in full swing. The Amtrak riders on the turbo train likely won't be reading books or doing crossword puzzles today. This photo was taken from the Bear Mountain Bridge, looking north. Manitou, NY, October 1986

BELOW: A single Budd RDC is southbound under the Bear Mountain Bridge in pre-Metro North days. The equipment was lettered MTA (Metropolitan Transportation Authority) and operated under contract by Conrail. It's a long climb down from Route 6 / 202, and at about the half way point I tied off a long length of rope to assist in my descent and climb back to the top. Going down wasn't too bad, but I had a devil of a time climbing out, so I never attempted to duplicate that feat. Cortlandt Manor, NY, June 1979

ABOVE: A single FL-9 on the *Lake Shore Limited* was a rare occurrence, and was documented as it burst out of Bear Mountain Tunnel. This photo was taken from a boat, a super way to railfan the Hudson River Valley. Cortlandt Manor, NY, August 1990

BELOW: This photo location, just south of the Bear Mountain Bridge, required a very long walk in from Roa Hook in Peekskill. Climbing down from the roadway, as in the facing photo, was out of the question. It was a wonderfully clear day, and the walk along the riverbank was enjoyable. My long hike was rewarded; the *Lake Shore Limited* was on time and looking great! I would like to revisit this location today but access to Roa Hook has been cut off by two sets of fences and lots of No Trespassing signs. Cortlandt Manor, NY, June 1982

ABOVE: A pair of FL-9's are northbound at the base of Anthony's Nose as a paddle-wheel sightseeing boat heads south on the river. This view is looking south from the Bear Mountain Bridge. The River Line looks pretty quiet on the west side.   Cortlandt Manor, NY, May 1992

ABOVE: FL-9 2018 bursts out of Middle Tunnel on a northbound run to Poughkeepsie. The face of the tunnel has been reinforced with concrete and its bore has been enlarged. A shoo-fly on the river side bypassed the tunnel during the upgrade.   Cortlandt Manor, NY, August 1990

BELOW: Amtrak E-9 414, a former Union Pacific locomotive, along with a sister E9, is southbound through the curve at Roa Hook. This location was made famous by Ed Nowak, New York Central's company photographer, and Don Ball, one of the most accomplished rail photographers.   Cortlandt Manor, NY, August 1979

ABOVE: Metro North Railroad was a little more than a year old when this photo was taken. The southbound FL-9 sports the MTA paint scheme, and at that time still retained its Hancock air whistle. This location is one of many that became difficult to visit when access to the railroad at Roa Hook was closed. The buildings in the background on the other side of the river are on Iona Island.

Cortlandt Manor, NY, July 1984

BELOW: Conrail FL-9 5022 is southbound at Little Tunnel, about a mile and a half south of the bridge. Although others have told me they cannot visualize it, I always thought this tunnel has an owl-like face, with two large sunken eyes and a large tuft of vegetation for a nose.

Cortlandt Manor, NY, July 1979

ABOVE: A pair of F-40's, each wearing a different version of Amtrak's 3-stripe scheme, are in charge of the *Lake Shore Limited* as it negotiates the reverse curve just north of Roa Hook.   Cortlandt Manor, NY, September 1980

BELOW: This view at Roa Hook affords the photographer the full impact of the reverse curve. The track occupied by the RDC has just been replaced with welded rail. The track in the foreground is still jointed, but the new ribbon rail is on the ground, waiting to be installed. Note the jointed rail laying on both sides of the far track. The scenery is so alluring in this part of the valley that I suspect the conductor made many trips standing up front enjoying the view.   Cortlandt Manor, NY, September 1980

ABOVE: This photograph was taken from Bear Mountain State Park, on the west bank of the river. The tugboat is pushing six empty barges to an aggregate plant near Kingston, and is being overtaken by a speedboat on the river and Metro North on land. Foliage is at its peak.
Cortlandt Manor, NY, October 2004

BELOW: The late evening sun illuminates the nose of Amtrak FL-9 491, which was built as New Haven 2029. The train charges northbound through the Roa Hook area just north of the City of Peekskill, some of which can be seen in the background.
Cortlandt Manor, NY, May 1990

ABOVE: December 1980 into January 1981 was one of the coldest three weeks I can ever remember. I say this so my insurance company does not cancel my policy for being foolhardy. I have seen the reports of people falling through the ice, but I assure you it wasn't about to happen this day! I waited on a strong shelf of ice for this southbound MTA (pre-Metro North) push-pull, on the verge of freezing as solid as the ice I was standing on, until the train came into sight. I never figured out if the engineer in the B23-7 was waving in appreciation of a photographer so dedicated, or if he was yelling "Get off of the ice, you huckleberry"! Either way, I didn't wait around for another train.
Peekskill, NY, January 1981

BELOW: A *Lake Shore Limited* of early Amtrak days consisting of all Heritage cars is led by a pair of E-9's. No. 48 is seen gliding through a curve at "Peekskill Rocks" (a local moniker), a location no longer accessible to railfan photographers. Peekskill, NY, May 1979

ABOVE: I heard the roar of an EMD approaching the rock cut as I got out of my car, so I ran to get a closer shot of a train coming through the cut. I had no idea if it would be the MTA commuter train (note that the FL-9 is still in Penn Central dress) or the Amtrak train; both were due about that time. To my shock and amazement, I found both racing southbound through the cut. The Dutch door on the fluted-side coaches allows the conductor to offer a friendly wave to the Amtrak crew. You can't plan a shot like this; you just have to be there when it happens.
Cortlandt Manor, NY, July 1979

BELOW: A fledging Metro North Commuter Railroad leased several units from NJ Transit, among them E-8A 4326. In spite of its NJT markings, the EMD was very familiar with this territory, having been built as New York Central 4083. A leased Amtrak E-unit brings up the rear on this push-pull commuter run.
Peekskill, NY, May 1984

ABOVE: We witness #48, the *Lake Shore Limited,* at "Peekskill Rocks". By the 1980's, Amfleet cars have encroached into the consist and a pair of FL-9's have replaced the E-units.

Peekskill, NY, July 1983

BELOW: Eastbound Amtrak train 254 glides along the eastern shore of the river on one of those days that all of the weathermen categorize as "one of the ten best days of the year". The day lived up to its billing, and I regretted that the passenger coaches of the 1940's and 50's, with windows that opened, are no longer used.

Peekskill, NY, May 2008

ABOVE: Equipped with a pair of knee-high boots at low tide enabled me to step off of "Peekskill Rocks" and grab this unusual shot of FL-9 488 leading the *Maple Leaf* north. Sounds like great planning doesn't it? Well, I waded too deep and the boots filled with water, which made it impossible to climb back onto the rocks. Not everything always goes as planned, but I did get the shot!   Peekskill, NY, October 1985

BELOW: A Metro North inspection train is southbound along the Hudson River at "Peekskill Rocks". Bringing up the rear is a real touch of class, one of the former DL&W Phoebe Snow tavern lounge cars!   Peekskill, NY, September 1989

ABOVE: Before we leave "Peekskill Rocks" I want to share one more shot with you. It was one of those mild fall days, and the sun and foliage were both cooperating. The Amtrak turbo is southbound.

Peekskill, NY, October 1993

ABOVE: A pair of E-8's, one from Amtrak and one from NJ Transit, are in the pull-pull mode on this northbound Metro North mid-day train.
Peekskill, NY, May 1984

BELOW: A shoo-fly around the Annsville Creek bridge has been built during reconstruction. The train will pull into the Peekskill station in about three minutes.
Peekskill, NY, May 1996

ABOVE: Friends looking at this photo accused me of staging it. It was not. Looking for all the world like "Dashing Dan", the logo of the Long Island Rail Road, this tardy commuter pleaded with the train crew to give him another minute. They did, and he made his train.
Peekskill, NY, March 1984

BELOW: NJ Transit E-8 4248 waits at the Peekskill station for the conductor to give the "OK to proceed" signal. The ornate station portico has been preserved by enclosing it and turning that part of the station into a tavern and restaurant
Peekskill, NY, May 1984

ABOVE: Amtrak train 248 had a turbo set assigned to it this day. The brick buildings behind the train are part of the former Fleischmann's Distillery complex at Peekskill. Aside from whisky, the company produced yeast and vinegar. Fleischmanns used a Porter fireless cooker at this location to switch their plant, which produced steam as a byproduct of the distilling process. The locomotive would be attached to a steam pipe from the plant and its huge chamber would be charged with steam. It would then switch cars for several hours, depending on the ambient temperature, before going back for another charge of steam.   Peekskill, NY, January 1994

BELOW: This was a favorite photo location of mine until the town condemned the one building on the east side of the bridge, and then fenced off the bridge itself. The brick buildings, although a couple of miles from the main plant, were also part of the Fleischmann's Distillery. The large white building is a garbage to energy power plant. The path of Route 6 / 202, cut into the mountainside leading to the Bear Mountain Bridge, can also be seen.   Buchanan, NY, December 1989

ABOVE: It doesn't get any prettier than this. Those are not FL-9's, but instead a pair of F-10's. All of those very fragrant bushes were removed when the restaurant was built in the station. This area is now alfresco dining and a huge favorite of kids of all ages who like to watch the trains go by. Peekskill, NY, July 1994

BELOW: This was a very cold January morning after back-to-back snow storms, followed by a deep freeze. You could walk on the crust of the snow without breaking through. That resulted in a lot of frozen switches and slow orders for the next several days. In spite of that, the *Maple Leaf* was on time. Peekskill, NY, January 1994

ABOVE: The *Niagara Rainbow* is seen southbound running opposite main. This view is from the stairs of the former Metro North Crugers station. Crugers and Montrose stations were razed, and a new complex was built at Cortlandt Manor to replace them. All of those beautiful signal bridges were razed when Metro North switched from lineside to cab signals. Crugers, NY, October 1992

ABOVE: F-10's 413 and 410 are on the rear and pushing this Metro North train southbound. The wooden-planked bridge that this shot was taken from has since been closed and fenced off.
Crugers, NY, July 1994

BELOW: Amtrak train 48, the *Lake Shore Limited,* is about to glide through Oscawanna Tunnel in Cortlandt Manor, NY. FL-9 #486 has a mix of standard and Amfleet cars in the consist on this day.
Oscawanna, NY, October 1991

ABOVE: This was the big event in the east during 1993. The new X-2000 train, designed and built in Sweden by A-B-B, was testing throughout the east on both electrified and non-electrified trackage. This was to be Amtrak's entree into the next generation of high speed rail service on the Northeast Corridor. Although the X-2000 would not be faster than Amtrak's Metroliner-electric MU's, the Swedish trains featured a.c. propulsion, radial trucks and a hydraulic body tilt system. On this day, the X-2000 ran from Rochester, NY, to Grand Central Station. It is seen passing through Oscawanna Tunnel, in non-electrified territory.   Oscawanna, NY, May 1993

BELOW: A set of turbos were painted in this unique scheme, utilized to power the X-2000 train in non-electrified zones.
                                                                                    Oscawanna, NY, May 1993

ABOVE: During the 1970's and 80's, the shop crews at Croton-Harmon would tell you that the Budd RDC's were the most reliable equipment on the railroad. This is a northbound RDC about to plunge into Oscawanna Tunnel. Looking farther south you can see the pedestrian foot bridge where Oscawanna Station once stood. Oscawanna, NY, October 1981

BELOW: Amtrak E-8 495, on lease to Metro North, leads a two car-mid-day train south. Originating in Poughkeepsie, this train will terminate at Croton-Harmon and passengers will walk across the platform to board a waiting train of M-1 electric MU cars to continue south. Oscawanna, NY, January 1984

ABOVE: P-32AC 713, one of eighteen Genesis units equipped for dual mode to accommodate third rail, exits Oscawanna Tunnel on its journey south to New York City. Its bashed-in nose not withstanding, the #713 sports the most attractive paint scheme Amtrak ever developed.
Oscawanna, NY, January 2004

BELOW: There is a lot going on in this photo. An evening rush-hour Metro North train exits the north portal of Oscawanna Tunnel led by FL-9's 2021 and 2007. Looking through the tunnel you can see a southbound Amtrak turbo that has just passed the fisherman and his girl-friend who are stumbling back to their car for more beer, having already discarded six empty cans on the banks of the river. The garbage left behind by fishermen sometimes reaches epic proportions and requires a clean up by railfan photographers who wish to include the shoreline in their photographs.
Oscawanna, NY, June 1995

ABOVE: B23-7 806, formerly Conrail 1908, was the first of the GE's to be painted by Metro North. It is pictured here showing off its new paint job as it works on the rear end of a northbound pull-pull commuter run, about to enter the tunnel.   Oscawanna, NY, October 1983

ABOVE: Amtrak P32-AC 706 bursts out of Oscawanna Tunnel with a Heritage baggage car on the head end. Train 49 is headed to Chicago along the Water Level Route.
Oscawanna, NY, May 2007

ABOVE: This is the most recognizable consist of the *Lake Shore Limited* during the 1980's: an F-40 (339) and FL-9 (487). The F-40 will come off four miles south at Croton Harmon and the FL-9 will continue on to Grand Central Terminal.　　Oscawanna, NY, October 1983

BELOW: This was one of those cold March days when there was nothing you could do to get warm. A strong wind off of the river penetrated all the layers of clothing you thought would make this morning bearable. It was my birthday! What the heck was I thinking? I should have been home in bed, but now I'm glad I wasn't.　　Cortlandt Manor, NY, March 1984

ABOVE: Metro North P32AC 222 is kicking up a lot of freshly fallen snow as it makes it way north from Croton-Harmon to Poughkeepsie. All of the electronics in the undercarriage of the big GE locomotive fare exceptionally well in inclement conditions.

Cortlandt Manor, NY, December 2005

BELOW: Another cold morning and another rock outcropping to climb. On the other side of the Hudson is Stony Point, NY. The conductor standing in the front of the car, has spotted the guy with the camera perched high above the track. He no doubt had seen me before.

Cortlandt Manor, NY, November 1980

ABOVE: This photograph exudes a sense of motion. It is surely an optical illusion, but the front of this Bomb cab-control car appears to be canted forward as if leaning into its work. The Connecticut State Seal on the front and the red stripe identify this car as belonging to ConnDOT. These cars, and New York State cars, are regularly intermixed when trains are being assembled.

Oscawanna, NY, December 2005

BELOW: Pretty as a picture ! A pair of FL-9's lean hard into a sweeping curve on this southbound run. That's Route 9 in the background, and the lead into Conrail's Croton West Yard in the foreground. Croton on Hudson, NY, September 2000

ABOVE: Earlier in this chapter I talked about being in the right place at the right time. That was the situation pictured here. The day was getting late, and it gets dark early during January in the Northeast. I watched as the Metro North SPV-2000's and the Amtrak Turbotrain (the *Adirondack*) raced each other southbound toward me. I knew because of the fading light that this would be the last shot of the day. As I shot the two southbound trains I heard a noise behind me and when I turned, there was Amtrak train 77, the *Hudson Highlander* splitting the two southbounds. If only the FL-9 had its headlight illuminated! Cortlandt Manor, NY, January 1986

BELOW: It's mid-day and it has been snowing since dawn as a pair of Metro North FL-9's set out from Croton-Harmon on a northbound run. The dwarf signals protect the non-electrified freight lead on the south end of Croton West Yard.
Croton-on-Hudson, NY, December 1992

ABOVE: P32-AC 707, a dual-mode Genesis unit, has the *Maple Leaf* on time as it accelerates out of Croton. This location affords a view right down the Hudson.

Croton-on-Hudson, NY, August 1998

BELOW: One set of Amtrak's turbos was rebuilt in the early 1990's and repainted into a scheme that looks like motion even when it's standing still. This train was not standing still, and it was due into Croton Harmon in two minutes. It would arrive right on the money. Looking across the river to the far left you can see the Conrail right of way cut into the hillside as it gains elevation from water level.

Croton-on-Hudson, NY, May 1996

ABOVE: A trio of Amtrak E-8's sporting two different paint schemes have train 48, the eastbound *Lake Shore Limited,* in tow past the former Croton West platform. So much at this location has changed since this photograph was made that it would be unrecognizable today. All of the buildings on the waterfront have been razed in favor of a town park. The signal bridge, the platforms and the pedestrian overpass I was standing on are also history.   Croton-on-Hudson, NY, June 1979

BELOW: This is one of my all-time favorite photographs. I had chatted with the family who were on their way into New York City for a Broadway show. They huddled in the inadequate plexiglass shelter trying to keep warm until the arrival of their train, which in this case would take them a little more than a mile to Croton Harmon, where they would have to change trains. The Budd RDC's were always a welcome sight and a favorite of mine to photograph. I'm sure on this cold winter morning, that family was equally excited to see them too.   Croton-on-Hudson, NY, January 1980

ABOVE: A very heavy snowfall has prompted the Metro North shop forces to put a pair of back-to-back Genesis units on this train, a southbound from Poughkeepsie. The locomotives are pulling the train, which is usually in the push mode when travelling south. Hitting a snowbank with two Genesis units is a lot safer than with a cab control car. By positioning the units back-to-back, the power could be run around its train at either end of the run. I gained elevation for this photo by taking advantage of a huge snow pile constructed by Conrail forces when they cleared the access road to their yard. That's the former New York Central Croton West station in the background.

Croton-on-Hudson, NY, February 1996

BELOW: Conrail RS-3 5509, still in full Penn Central paint, is shoving a cut of former New Haven electric M.U.'s into the Croton West dead line. The 120-seat coaches, nicknamed "washboards," were built by Pullman-Standard, and were numbered in the 4400-series. Conrail, as did Metro North after them, used a dozen or so of the Washboards in commuter service on the Hudson and Harlem lines. The pantographs were left on the roof, and the third rail pick up shoes remained, in spite of the fact that the cars were pulled by diesels. This cut was going into storage with many sisters and a few FL-9's to make them feel at home. The great model railroad store that had occupied the station has moved out, and the windows are boarded up. A few years later, an architectural and electrical engineering firm would buy the building and completely refurbish it, even adding a pair of former DL&W MU "Edison Cars" for storage purposes.

Croton-on-Hudson, NY, August 1980

ABOVE: It was not all fun and games during the 1980's. A lot of the equipment that I loved to photograph just disappeared. However, the worst times were when they cut it up right in front of you. Alco/ GE S-Motor 4723 and four FL-9's will all see the scrapper's torch during the coming days. Croton West Yard, NY, August 1982

BELOW: FL-9 5035, the only number it ever wore after its New Haven Railroad days, has fallen victim to high scrap prices. The scrapper's crane is about to lift out its EMD 567-C prime mover. Having endured open heart surgery myself, I can say I know the feeling. S-Motors, New Haven "washboard" electric MU's and former New York Central 1100-series MU's would all meet the same fate in a scrapping frenzy at this site. Croton West Yard, NY, August 1982

ABOVE: Jointed rail, overhead lineside signals, and even some wooden insulator strips on the third rail all conspire to date this photograph. FL-9 5020 leads a southbound mid-afternoon train south. It has just passed CD tower and will be at its assigned platform at Croton Harmon in less than five minutes. In my opinion, that is the most attractive paint scheme ever worn by an FL-9. It gives the locomotive the appearance of puffing out its chest and holding its head high!
Croton-on-Hudson, NY, September 1981

BELOW: There is activity on 48 track. S-Motor 4715 is about to deliver an M-1 car to the shop electricians. There are still many 1100-series MU's in the stalls, along with the much newer M-1's. A Budd RDC, sunning itself on 50 track, and a former New Haven "washboard" showing the scars of its pantograph amputation, round out this early 1980's scene at the iconic Croton-Harmon Shops.
Croton-Harmon, NY, June 1981

ABOVE: "Number 48 is on the bell". That was the message from CD tower to the shop forces at Croton-Harmon, alerting them to the arrival of the *Lake Shore Limited*. It's mid-December and still very mild as three F-40's (3,000 HP each) come to a stop at their designated location, about 1,000 feet north of the station platform. A member of the shop crew is already in place to yank on the uncoupling lever that will separate the locomotives from their train. An Amtrak FL-9 is standing by to couple on and deliver the train to the Croton-Harmon platform. After that station stop, the train will operate nonstop until it reaches Grand Central Terminal, in about an hour and five minutes.

Croton-Harmon, NY, December 1979

BELOW: One of the conductors has stepped out of the train and appears to be timing the engine change. One of the shop crew is doffing his hard hat as a signal to the engineer in FL-9 488 to "come back to a hitch". In about two minutes they will be on their way.

Croton-Harmon, NY, December 1979

ABOVE: During the Conrail era of running the commuter lines, some very interesting equipment made appearances, not least of which was a train of former Delaware & Hudson coaches. This was one of the prettiest passenger trains Conrail ever ran, because the D&H cars perfectly matched the Conrail paint scheme on the FL-9's. This train has just left the Croton-Harmon station on a southbound run to Grand Central Terminal.

Croton-Harmon, NY, July 1981

BELOW: During the 1970's and 80's the shop forces at Croton-Harmon were very tolerant of railfan photographers at the south end of the shop tracks. I suspect that this was even more so if they had seen you before. I can attest that they had seen me many times and knew who I was. Here a hostler has a two car-two FL-9- train that was being readied for the evening Croton-Harmon to Poughkeepsie run. After exchanging a few pleasantries, he was off to the fuel rack. I wonder if we will ever see those days again in this post-911 paranoia?

Croton-Harmon, NY, December 1980

ABOVE: Metro North GP-9 750 (ex-Conrail 7508, *nee*-New York Central 5935) is fresh out of the paint shop, shedding Conrail blue for Metro North paint. The 750 was the only GP-9 that Metro North had that was equipped with a steam heat generator, even though it did not work in passenger service.   Croton-Harmon, NY, May 1992

BELOW: This is my favorite shot of the Conrail S-Motors. Still in Penn Central dress, the 4725 sits in the backshop, its duties honorably completed, waiting to be scrapped. I'm glad I was there to preserve her memory before she met her fate   Croton-Harmon, NY, August 1979

ABOVE: Former Niagara Junction E10-B electric locomotives 4750 (nee NJ 14) and 4753 (nee NJ 17) built by General Electric sit in the backshop at Croton-Harmon. They have been repainted for the MTA (pre Metro North). They were purchased by the MTA primarily for switching in Grand Central Terminal. Visible in the rear is Conrail B23-7 2806 with extensive front end damage. On November 7, 1980, 2806 was northbound at Dobbs Ferry, NY, with train OPSE (Bronx, NY to Selkirk, NY) when it collided head-on with southbound Amtrak train #74, a turbo set.   Croton-Harmon, NY, December 1980

BELOW: Croton-Harmon has always been an interesting place for railfan photographers, dating back to the days when New York Central Hudsons rode the turntable. While the Hudsons might have stolen the show, there was also a variety of smaller steam and electric locomotives of every possible configuration and shape. This is where steam locomotives from places like Chicago, Indianapolis and Buffalo were taken off their trains and replaced with an array of electric locomotives for the remainder of their journey south (east by the timetable) into electrified territory. In the next several photos we will take advantage of the hospitality of Conrail and Metro North and explore in and around Croton-Harmon, starting with this Long Island Railroad Alco C-420, 225, on lease to Metro North during the mid-eighties. Both railroads are owned by the Metropolitan Transit Authority.   Croton-Harmon, NY, August 1985

ABOVE: Metro North FL-9 2024 poses for a portrait at the backshop. Ditch lights, MU receptacles and Nathan horns replacing the Hancock Air Whistle are among the most obvious changes since the New Haven Railroad took delivery of this locomotive in 1960 as 2058.

Croton-Harmon, NY, March 2006

BELOW: A new locomotive for Metro North. Brookville Equipment Co. of Brookville, Pennsylvania, has been building very small mining and industrial locomotives since 1918. When Metro North decided to replace several well-worn former Niagara Junction E-10B switchers, they gave Brookville Equipment their first opportunity to build two full sized locomotives. The result was this model BL-06, a 70 ton, 600 horsepower unit delivered in 2001.

Croton-Harmon, NY, July 2006

ABOVE: A helicopter view of the backshop of Metro North's Harmon Shops. Two FL-9's, a Brookville BL-06, and M-7 and M-3 MU sets account for the rail equipment in this photo. The shops were constructed by the New York Central Railroad between 1906 and 1913. The main shop is 448 feet long, and the entire complex exceeds 200 acres. There are many inaccurate stories circulating about the origin of the Harmon name. Most believe that a Village of Harmon once existed on the land now occupied by the shops. Not so. In 1903, a very successful local real estate developer named Clifford Harmon sold the land for the shops to the railroad with one stipulation; that anything built on that land would forever bear his name. So be it!

Croton-Harmon, NY, March 2007

RIGHT: The day is quickly turning into evening as Metro North Genesis 230 is attended to at the Harmon fuel rack

Croton-Harmon, NY, June 2004

ABOVE: Yet another model for Metro North. In 1993 the railroad took delivery of six former Conrail, *nee*-Reading (note the telltale rain gutter over the cab window) rebuilt GP-35's. The 101 has just been delivered, and it arrived without even getting its trucks dirty! The GP-35's are painted into Metro North's MOW scheme, and are used primarily on work trains.   Croton-Harmon, NY, December 1993

BELOW: Metro North FL-9 2005 leads F7-A 417, on lease from the United Railroad Historical Society of New Jersey, to the wash shed. The 417 was donated to the URHS after working for a few years on NJ Transit. It was built as Chicago & North Western 4073C. In the background is the venerable diesel and electric shops constructed between 1906 and 1913 by the New York Central Railroad. This photo required a tree climb, and some branch trimming, much to the amusement of several Metro North employees.

Croton-Harmon, NY, May 1992

ABOVE: If they would have asked me, I would have said this is how all of the FL-9's should have been painted! No. 2012 was one of two FL-9's repainted by Metro North to honor its New York Central heritage, and is posed at the backshop during one of the Metro North's open house events at the Croton-Harmon shops.

Croton-Harmon, NY, November 1999

BELOW: Dewitt rebuilt Alco RS-3m 605 was the resident Croton-Harmon switcher for several years. It eventually became the only MNRR locomotive without cab signals on the Hudson Division, and therefore, did not leave Harmon yard. It was later transferred to Metro North's Connecticut lines (at least on paper), which accounts for the ConnDOT decal. Built as Delaware, Lackawanna & Western 912, it is now preserved as part of the Danbury Railway Museum collection in Danbury, Connecticut.

Croton-Harmon, NY, May 1999

ABOVE: In 1991 seven FL-9 locomotives were rebuilt by Asea-Brown-Boveri at Republic Locomotive. They emerged as FL-9AC's, with new AC traction motors and a turbocharged power plant that produced 3,000 HP, almost double the original 1750 HP output. That was the good news. The bad news was that for most of their short-lived careers, the "Starships" as they were called by Metro North personnel, because of all of their advanced electronics, sat exactly where they are pictured here, at the backshop. The unreliable "new" beast was universally despised by train crews and shop forces alike. If you wanted to get on the bad side of a shop employee, just ask him "How are your Starships doing?" Metro North FL-9AC 2040 is pictured with a pair lettered for sister Long Island Railroad. A shop foreman once told me "We wanted to send all seven to the LIRR, but they were too smart for that". All seven were eventually scrapped.

Croton-Harmon, NY, February 1992

BELOW: I got the call one evening that Metro North had decided on a paint scheme, and the first unit had been painted. I hurried down to the shops to find FL-9 5033 in a red, blue and silver scheme. "The paint isn't dry yet, we will roll it outside tomorrow" I was told.

Croton-Harmon, NY, June 1983

116

ABOVE: Open House visitors to Croton Shop get a hands-on tour of most of the equipment. They get to sit in the engineer's seat and try it out, as the author's wife and granddaughter are doing in a recently-rebuilt 1100-series MU car.   Croton-Harmon, NY, November 1985

ABOVE: Amtrak F-40 338 has its work cut out for it, if it is to reach its final destination, Grand Central Terminal. A 24-inch snowfall has just crippled New York State from Buffalo to New York City, but 338 made like a snow plow and somehow arrived at Croton-Harmon not more than an hour behind schedule, quite commendable given the conditions.   Croton-Harmon, NY, February 1983

BELOW: A brace of five SPV-2000's are heading into the shop area. I don't know what the occasion was that precipitated this movement, but it wasn't something that normally occurred. It was, however, just another interesting sight in and around the Harmon Shops.
Croton-Harmon, NY, July 1987

ABOVE: A pair of FL-9's lead a train comprised of SEMTA (South East Michigan Transit Authority) coaches past the infamous Sing Sing Prison and into the station at Ossining. The term "going up the river" was engendered by persons who were convicted of crimes in New York City and then sent, sometimes via the New York Central Railroad, up the river to Ossining's Sing Sing Prison.

Ossining, NY, July 1985

BELOW: A northbound Amtrak turbo races along the shore of the Hudson River, with the Tappan Zee Bridge looming in the background. Tappan was the name of a small tribe of local Indians, and Zee is the Dutch word for sea or a large expanse of water. This is the widest section of the Hudson River; the bridge is more than three miles long. When Henry Hudson found this wide expanse in September 1609, he believed that he had found the northwest passage. One of the central themes of this book, as outlined in the introduction, is "you can't take that picture today. Things have changed." You can't take this shot at North Tarrytown anymore, because North Tarrytown no longer exists. In 1996 the town changed its name to the moniker given it by author Washington Irving, Sleepy Hollow.

North Tarrytown, NY, September 1991

ABOVE: Train 238 is in third rail territory with the Tappan Zee Bridge spanning the river in the background. Notice the lighthouse on the far left-hand side of the span.

Sleepy Hollow, NY, April 2008

BELOW: Former New Haven Railroad 4400 series "washboard" MU's, accustomed to stretching their pantographs to reach overhead wires, are now running on third rail. The large building in the background with the two tall stacks is a former New York Central coal-fired powerhouse that supplied electricity to the direct-current third rail system. The pedestrian overpass at the Glenwood Station can be seen beyond the roadway bridge.

Yonkers, NY, June 1983

ABOVE: P32-AC 703 leads an Amtrak train north past the Tarrytown General Motors Assembly Plant that was opened in 1914. Just two months after this photograph was taken, the plant rolled out its last vehicle and closed its doors forever. A year and a half later there was no sign the plant had ever existed, as all buildings were razed. North Tarrytown, NY, May 1996

BELOW: By the Millennium Year the Amtrak turbo trains had received a new paint scheme. In this view from the Babcock Place bridge we see a northbound set (going away from the camera). In the background is the former Phelps-Dodge Copper Plant, which at the time of the photo, was a large movie studio. Yonkers has been called "Hollywood on the Hudson" because of all of the Movies and television shows shot there. Yonkers, NY, September 2000

ABOVE: Metro North P32-AC 207 leads a train northward through downtown Yonkers. In the background is the "Home of the Elevator", the former Otis Elevator complex, now an industrial park. Beyond that, and sandwiched between the steeple of St. Mary's Church and the bullet shaped dome of City Hall, is 30 South Broadway, which in addition to its many offices, once housed the northern terminus of the Getty Square Branch of the New York Central's Putnam Division. Yonkers, NY, November 2001

BELOW: This photograph was taken from the third floor of the former trolley barn of the Third Avenue Trolley System. A southbound-early morning Amtrak train is making a station stop at the beautiful Beaux Arts-style station that was constructed in 1911. In the background is the world famous Palisades on the New Jersey side of the Hudson. Yonkers, NY, March 2001

ABOVE: Amtrak train 239 is northbound through Yonkers at exactly 6:00 p.m., and it's still almost 100 degrees on the day before the Fourth of July. It was no time to be standing on the tarred roof of a high-rise, but the vantage point was too enticing. Directly behind the train is the Jack Frost Sugar refinery, and in the foreground several covered hoppers waiting to be switched into the plant for outbound loads. Down-river is the George Washington Bridge and the New York City skyline.   Yonkers, NY, July 2003

BELOW: Amtrak FL-9 486 has the *Lake Shore Limited* gliding through the Spuyten Duyvil section of the northern Bronx. The high arched bridge supports the two levels of the Henry Hudson Parkway, while the open swing bridge portends the future re-routing of all Amtrak trains into Penn Station instead of Grand Central Terminal.   The Bronx, NY, March 1991

ABOVE: Metro North FL-9 2005 leads a mid-day train through the very tight Spuyten Duyvil rock cut. In the background is the Broadway Bridge, which carries vehicular traffic and the IRT elevated subway between Manhattan and the Marble Hill section of The Bronx. The bridge spans the Harlem River, a tributary of the Hudson. The Bronx, NY, March 1991

ABOVE: New York City is electrified territory and home to multiple units (MU's). While many railfan photographers shun these trains, they are part of the railroad landscape. These are the trains that move millions of passengers each year. Here a train of M-7 MU's is seen pulling into the Spuyten Duyvil station in The Bronx. The mighty Palisades form the backdrop at this location. The Bronx, NY, November 2008

BELOW: I am standing on the Manhattan side of the Broadway Bridge over the Harlem River for this photo of a set of M-7's pulling into the Marble Hill station in the Bronx. The shadow in the river is that of the lift bridge on which I am standing. It carries vehicles and pedestrians on the main level, and the Broadway line of the IRT subway overhead. My previous attempt at this shot was unsuccessful because of a passing subway train that caused vibration that was reflected in the photograph. Marble Hill, Bronx, NY, November 2008

ABOVE: A Metro North string of MU's is framed by the Roman Arches of the High Bridge Aqueduct. Constructed between 1837 and 1848 it delivers water to Manhattan as part of the forty-one mile long Old Croton Aqueduct, the oldest system in the United States. The bronze lettering on the column lists the architects and engineers responsible for building the aqueduct. Most prominent among the names is James Renwick, who started his career as a structural engineer with the Eire Railroad and went on to design several world famous buildings that include New York's St. Patricks Cathedral and the Smithsonian Institution.   The Bronx, NY, June 1983

BELOW: FL-9 486 has the *Lake Shore Limited* on time through the High Bridge section of The Bronx. I am standing on the former roadbed of the New York Central's Putnam Division. The arch bridge in the background was designed to resemble a Roman aqueduct, but the stone arches over the Harlem River had to be replaced by a steel structure in the 1920's.   The Bronx, NY, September 1982

ABOVE: The Mott Haven section of The Bronx once housed large yards where New York Central and New Haven passenger cars were stored. It is also the junction where the Central's Hudson and Harlem lines merged for the final leg of the journey south into Grand Central Terminal. In 1991, before Metro North instituted cab signaling, little had changed, except that the layover yards were no longer there. This southbound Amtrak turbo is coming in from the Hudson Line, having just passed Yankee Stadium, while a set of M-4 MU's head north on the Harlem Line.   The Bronx, NY, March 1991

BELOW: This is a view of the 138th Street lift bridge that spans the Harlem River. FL-9s 2008 and 2030 are pushing hard and will make their next station stop, 125th Street in Harlem, in a matter of minutes.   The Bronx, NY, March 1991

ABOVE: Train 63, the *Maple Leaf* is about twelve minutes out of Grand Central Terminal and northbound over the 138th Street lift bridge for one of the last times. Within a month, Amtrak would activate the West Side Connector (also known as the "Empire Connection") from the swing bridge at Spuyten Duyvil into Penn Station, via the west side of Manhattan. For this day, however, Amtrak's patrons were able to enjoy the grandeur of Grand Central Terminal !
The Bronx, NY, March 1991

OPPOSITE TOP: A set of MU's race along the Park Ave Viaduct in Harlem and are about to duck into the tunnel at 97th Street. The remainder of the trip into Grand Central Terminal will be underground. The commuters who ride these trains every day have already closed their books and newspapers, and will hit the platform at New York speed (considered running in other parts of the country) when the train comes to a halt.
Manhattan, NY, March 1991

OPPOSITE BOTTOM: For safety reasons, photography on the platforms of Grand Central Terminal was discouraged long before the events of 911. Prior permission was granted by Metro North Police for this shot of FL-9 2014 resting in the terminal between runs.
Manhattan, NY, February 1988

The Hudson Line
Freight Service

Two major yards anchor the freight traffic on the Hudson Line. Oak Point Yard in the South Bronx receives traffic from upstate New York and either transloads it to trucks for local delivery or redirects the carloads across the Hell Gate Bridge into Long Island. On the other end of the equation is Selkirk Yard near Albany. Today CSX runs one train in each direction during the early morning hours. Each train makes a stop at Croton-West Yard to pick up and drop off cars during the dead of the night. Conrail, on the other hand, ran their two trains during the daylight hours and presented photographic opportunities in the lower Hudson Valley. One other railroad has trackage rights on the Hudson Line. The Canadian Pacific, through its subsidiary the Delaware & Hudson Railway, obtained trackage rights from the Albany, NY area (Kenwood Yard) to Fresh Pond Junction in Queens. The CP may pick up and deliver cars at Fresh Pond Jct., but may not service customers anywhere else on the line.

ABOVE: A pair of Conrail B23-7's lead OPSE through the rock cut at Roa Hook. The city of Peekskill can be seen in the background.
Peekskill, NY, February 1994

ABOVE: A trio of U30-B's and an SW-1500 have Conrail train SEOP (Selkirk to Oak Point in the Bronx, NY) passing Breakneck Mountain on their southbound run. During the tenure of Conrail, there were daylight road freights on the Hudson Line. Cold Spring, NY, June 1979

BELOW: This is the same train and same location as in the facing photograph. However, this time the temperature is about sixty degrees warmer. Also note that the U30-B's are running on the "wrong main".   Peekskill, NY, August 1979

ABOVE: CSX forged an agreement with Metro North to run its two road freights in the wee early hours of the morning. They do however, run locals both north and south out of Croton West yard in daylight. This train had a GP40-2 on either end to facilitate switching moves. CSX 6207 is pulling south, long hood forward, past the Manitou wetlands. The Hudson River is on the other side of the train.   Manitou, NY, February 2003

BELOW: A trio of B23-7's lead a rather short train north across the Peekskill causeway. The three GE's are less than three years old and their fairly new paint looks good in the mid-day sun. I was disappointed when I did not see a caboose on the rear of the train until I saw the jade green New York Central box car bringing up the markers.   Peekskill, NY, March 1980

ABOVE: B23-7 1943 is northbound through Manitou on a unseasonably warm and humid November morning with a train of predominantly box car traffic. The Bear Mountain Bridge can be seen in the background.   Manitou, NY, November 1989

BELOW: A late afternoon SEOP is southbound along Peekskill Bay. Just before the tide in the river changes, the water gets very placid. It appears that the high tide is about to change as there is not the slightest splash along the shoreline.   Peekskill, NY, March 1983

ABOVE: The foliage is starting to turn as this northbound races along the Metro North Hudson Line through Westchester County. This is a mid-day train that maintained a tight schedule as not to interfere with passenger service. The consist is mostly empty boxcars that carried auto parts to the Tarrytown GM plant, and empty reefers. The track on the far right is the lead into Conrail's Croton West yard.
Cortlandt Manor, NY, September 1983

BELOW: Viewing a train from the height of the rail is a somewhat different perspective. This mid-afternoon southbound still employs a hack on the rear, and two members of the train crew are doing a little sightseeing on this warm summer day.   Peekskill, NY, June 1980

ABOVE: Freshly painted B23-7's 1934 and 2802 lead an Office Car Special south through Peekskill, enroute to the General Motors assembly plant at North Tarrytown, NY. On board are Conrail and state officials, and GM executives, all of whom will share the podium at the GM plant to proclaim their support for the plant and the traffic it generates for Conrail. Unfortunately, exactly six years later, the plant will close its doors forever.   Peekskill, NY, July 1990

BELOW: This is the "Salad Bowl Express," one of several SEOP trains out of Selkirk yard, with refrigerated cars that originated in the fertile valleys of California. The train is loaded with lettuce, broccoli, tomatoes and other fresh produce destined for the Hunts Point Terminal Market in the South Bronx, less than a mile from Oak Point yard, the train's eastern terminus. It is pictured exiting the south portal of Oscawanna Tunnel on a day when the ambient temperature is colder than inside the refrigerated cars.   Oscawanna, NY, February 2004

ABOVE: This is a wonderful photo and I'm glad I was there to make it. Just a first generation U-boat switching some cars? Upon closer inspection you will find that the U25-B is switching an entire string of vintage box cars untouched by graffiti. Isn't that a pretty sight?

Croton-on-Hudson, NY, November 1981

BELOW: The engineer in Conrail B23-7 1918 is focused on his switching assignment in Croton West Yard and does not give so much as a glance at the Amtrak turbo train speeding by on the main. His heavy jacket and gloves are an indication of early winter

Croton-on-Hudson, NY, November 1979

ABOVE: That is quite a train you have there sir! Conrail B23-7 2021 and several sisters are poised to take an exceptionally long version of OPSE north to Selkirk. The bulk of the train came north from Oak Point during the night, and several cars were added at the Croton West Yard. Conrail dispatchers will get the train north of Poughkeepsie before the start of the evening commuter rush.

Croton-on-Hudson, NY, February 1997

BELOW: It's early evening and three GE U30-B's have the "Salad Bowl Express" roaring past the Croton West station platform. No. 2879 (formerly NYC #2879) is still in full Penn Central paint. By midnight workers at the Hunts Point Terminal Market will already be unloading some of those reefers.

Croton-on-Hudson, NY, April 1979

ABOVE: SW-1001's are obviously the switcher of choice at the yard in 1988. Two of the EMD's have a train ready to go south with box cars for the GM plant, while the remaining two will stay behind to switch the yard. Over the years, Conrail assigned various switcher fleets to the Croton West yard, including SW-1500's and GP-9's.   Croton West Yard, NY, November 1979

BELOW: The snow has tapered off considerably in the last twenty minutes, and the crew, who has switching chores at North Tarrytown, Irvington and Yonkers, hopes it stays that way.   Croton West Yard, NY, February 1993

ABOVE: "If you want to play with your trains today you first have to shovel the snow". I bet a lot of youngsters can relate to that. There are fourteen inches of snow covering those switches, and after they have been shoveled clean, B36-7 5830 will grind over them a time or two to ensure that the flangeways are clear.   Croton West Yard, NY, February 2003

BELOW: The torch has been passed. Conrail blue has disappeared in favor of CSX yellow and blue. The SW-1500's and SW-1001's are gone and B36-7 5839 has assumed the switching duties. The old Croton West station sill looks good doesn't it? Croton West Yard, NY, March 2000

ABOVE: The switches have been cleared and the CSX crew had made up the afternoon train that will work as far north as Poughkeepsie. A sister B36-7 on the other end of the train will facilitate switching moves and expedite the return trip to Croton-West after what was, no doubt, a long day for that crew.
Croton West Yard, NY, February 2003

BELOW: In 1984 Conrail experimented with the Roadrailer concept, running between the Bronx and Buffalo, NY. #2971, a U36-B is all the power this lightweight consist requires.
Ossining, NY, September 1984

ABOVE: A pair of B23-7's have a train of box cars for the GM plant as they races through the station at Scarborough, trying to put some distance between them and a following Metro North local that will stop and pick up the passengers who have been completely dusted with snow by the passing freight! Scarborough, NY, March 1989

BELOW: A pair of GP38-2's have a ten car train in tow southbound out of Croton-West Yard. The local, which is pictured passing the Senesqua Sailing School in Croton-on-Hudson, will deliver cars to Irvington, Yonkers and The Bronx. Croton-On-Hudson, NY, May 2008

ABOVE: A lone SW-1500 has a cut of cars that is comprised of empty box cars it just picked up at the GM plant, and covered hoppers that it will deliver to the Flo Sweet sugar refinery in Yonkers. That is the Tappan Zee Bridge in the background.   Tarrytown, NY, March 1981

BELOW: A pair of B23-7's out of the Croton West yard is hard at work, switching cars at the General Motors plant. The box cars contain various components of the Chevrolets that will be assembled there.   Tarrytown, NY, May 1996

ABOVE: Two CSX GP38-2's are running light at Spuyten Duyvil on their way to Oak Point Yard in the South Bronx to pick up north-bound cars. In the background is the world-famous Palisades. Amtrak's "Empire Connection" line into Penn Station diverges from the Metro North mainline at this location and runs past the abandoned brick tower.
The Bronx, NY, November 2008

BELOW: A string of B23-7's sit on the ready track at Oak Point yard. To the left, out of the photograph, is the approach to the famous Hell Gate Bridge that connects the Bronx, NY, with the boroughs of Queens and Brooklyn, as well as Long Island. This is a seedy area, and getting this and a couple other shots, and then getting safely out of town, rivaled any of the exploits I have described previously in this book.
The Bronx, NY, July 1990

The Author

The author's initial exposure to trains was at a pre-school age, when he would walk with his dad to the Yonkers, New York, city pier to watch New York Central trains pass by, as well as the coming and going of the Hudson River Dayliner excursion boats. It was still at an early age when he decided to make the trip one day on his own. As his frantic family and police searched the neighborhood for the missing lad, he was hoisted onto a baggage wagon by a station porter who assumed he belonged to one of the numerous families on the platform waiting for a train. When the police finally located him, he got his first ride in a police car, back to his waiting parents.

In 1969, Bill Mc Bride joined that very same Yonkers Police Department and was assigned a foot-patrol-post in the downtown business district from midnight to 8 a.m. Thirty-eight years later, he retired from the 620-man City Of Yonkers Police Department as Deputy Chief.

Bill has been married to his wife Suzanne for 43 years, a union which has produced three children; John, Kimberly and Bill; six grandchildren, and one great granddaughter.

Author Bill Mc Bride trackside in 2008. The photo was taken by 9-year old grandson Kevin Hettwer